Never Give Up

Never Give Up

James Farrin

IngramSpark

CONTENTS

CONTENTS

CONTENTS

To Marianne and my wonderful kids,
Jim, Jenny, Ray, Melody, and Jon

Introduction

The overarching theme of my memoir is "don't give up" and the importance of being open to different ideas as we navigate through life's phases, as we all need continuous growth. I am writing to share the significant lessons from my own life and to unveil growth possibilities for every person, irrespective of their circumstances. Initially, I hope readers will appreciate the joy of finding laughter in various situations, even those that may initially cause angst. The beauty of laughter lies in uncovering different ideas that not only bring joy but also open delightful pathways for both the young and old. In life, irrespective of the challenges we face, it is crucial to approach these situations with confidence and always allow for at least a second or even a third chance for success.

Sporting achievements have played a prominent role in my life, marked by instances such as beating Arthur Ashe 2-6, 7-5, 6-Love. Another significant episode was the paradoxical success of failing to win the National Father and Son Tennis

Tournament, where we consistently ranked as the second-best team in America.

I have encountered pivotal turning points, particularly in later years, revolving around health and maintaining a positive attitude in the face of extreme challenges. I aspire and plan for this memoir to deeply impact those seeking change in their lives. A surprising element is woven into my story, especially in my pursuit of a career as a professional comedian, which quickly fell short of my intentions.

Today, the most important aspects of my life revolve around individuals facing severe challenges during crucial times. These situations continue to broaden my perspective and inspire me to persevere in all circumstances if possible. The significant challenges center around encountering difficult situations that demand a positive outlook and faith, which, for me, comes from God. My aim is for readers to be captivated by the depth and extraordinary variability of my story, particularly impacting those at a crossroads in their lives.

Getting Started

I had an unruly start. My father served in the United States Navy and was stationed in the Pacific. Consequently, I attended 13 different schools in 12 years. Amidst the constant change, tennis emerged as my anchor. I was fortunate to have a world-class instructor guide me on the path to becoming an excellent tennis player. At the age of 14, my father and I became New England champions in the Father and Son Tennis Tournament. I vividly recall my father's post-victory ritual: "Jimmy, gather up your things quickly because there are a lot of people who watched and want to congratulate us." He instilled in me the significance of winning and the value of practicing religiously.

My father held me back from starting tennis until I was 13 years old. Notably, he had me hitting tennis balls late into the night, a spectacle in our neighborhood. From an early age, he impressed upon me the importance of winning, persevering, and occasionally, finding laughter. Many of his lessons stemmed from tremendous perseverance; I recall a singles match where he was down 6-Love, 5-Love, 40-Love, and miraculously won. When I expressed disbelief, he simply said, "You should never give up. If you remember this lesson and apply it, Jim, you are on your way." Tennis continued to open doors for me as we moved throughout the East Coast, but I grew restless, feeling I wasn't developing as I should.

My father secured admission for me to Philips Exeter Academy. However, I faced a setback when confronted with the competitive academic environment in 11th grade. My toughest teacher declared, "You may find this just too hard for you." My immediate response was a determined declaration: "I'm going to show you and others that I'm not just a tennis player." While the academic struggles at Philips Exeter Academy were real, my father dismissed any suggestion of going back a year. My French teacher, acknowledging my deficiency in academics, praised my tennis skills. I became a diligent student, navigating through the academic challenges.

Exeter had never won a national championship, and we were well on our way when I encountered a terrible pain that prevented me from completing the tournament, denying Exeter the national championship. This setback would prove to be a valuable life lesson in overcoming obstacles.

3

Early Surprises

I had a number of stumbles in my very early days. The first was a severe condition when I was ten years old, and I remember hearing a doctor whisper to my dad, "You know, he may not make it." My father said, "I have a trick I'm going to use, and I'll be praying for him." So, the trick was my dad put together a train set which went under the floor. When I saw it, I changed color; I was so excited because I always dreamed of having my own train set. I'd hear the train noises as my dad came back through, and I saw that the set was actually moving. Three weeks later, I was well, and the doctor said, "This is really a train miracle. He seems much better, and I think he's going to pull through."

One that I will always remember was an early match I played in the under 14 tournament, and I looked down at my knee, which was producing a lot of pain, and I could see the bone exposed. This time they called me the "medical marvel" because I had a rare disease called ostrich slaters, which attracted several people in the medical field who had never seen someone my age with ostrich slaters. The doctors did immediate surgery and were amazed at how anyone that young could contract such a rare condition.

Later, I had another bout in which I became paralytic due to a locked-in condition, which kept me from moving my retina. I became the hit of movies, who would see me crying away and quickly telling their friends, "Look at this man, he's laughing at this terrible movie." It was a little embarrassing. Luckily, I was able to get rid of that one, too. In a sense, it was like I had several examples of rare diseases, which served as an early introduction into painful problems. In my early time at Princeton, when people had difficult conditions to face, they would call me the "disease man" because I could sometimes make them laugh but always take them out of misery.

4

You'll Have to Take a
Year Off

At Exeter, I faced one of the most challenging English teachers imaginable, displaying an evident bias against me. I found myself thinking, "This guy must hate tennis players." During Thanksgiving vacation, I attempted to leverage my father's intellect with a few words and phrases. I still recall his words echoing in my ears, "Farrin, you didn't write this yourself, did you?" Stumped on how to respond, I finally admitted, "No, sir, I didn't write all those words myself. My father helped me on a few occasions." Subsequently, I was expelled from the class and summoned to meet him at the end of the school day. He emphatically declared that I was unfit to graduate and would need to repeat the grade. In defiance, I drew inspiration from my father's words, asserting, "You don't know me very well; I'm not someone who gives up easily. I will graduate with more than one honor." After the first year, when certain awards were given, I received recognition as the most improved student.

Upon confronting him, he declared, "I'm determined that you should take a year off from Exeter. I'm going to work very hard to make that happen." Undeterred, I retorted, "Well, I'm going to work very hard to get into Princeton University and visualize you sitting in the crowd when I win a big tennis match, working harder than anybody else in the school." Despite his expected negative response that people shouldn't set unattainable goals, I confidently said, "We will see." This marked a pivotal turning point, providing me with a seemingly impossible goal that, despite the tremendous effort required, reinstilled confidence and set me on a life-changing course.

Exeter had always aspired to have a national intercollegiate trophy in its cabinet. Graduating with a remarkable tennis partner, Dick Hoehn, we won the eastern regional championship, positioning ourselves well for the national trophy. With my #5 singles ranking and #1 doubles ranking, we were on the cusp of becoming national champions. I secured a major upset win over a higher-ranked opponent in a grueling match in boiling heat. However, that evening, a ferocious pain in my right leg surfaced, and the next morning, walking became difficult. Despite my tennis partner sobbing and my determination to play, a doctor's mandate requiring approval dashed our hopes of being national champions. The disappointment lingered, with my father acknowledging, "He'll never forget this as long as he lives, nor will Exeter Academy." Although it took time to overcome, three months later, I was back on the court, reigniting my dreams.

5

Princeton

Princeton had always been a dream of mine, boasting a stellar reputation across various domains, particularly in higher learning. This desire, in part, served as a testament to my English teacher that miracles, as he spoke of, could indeed happen. My unique background—attending 13 schools in 12 years all over the United States, coupled with a strong tennis history—opened doors and fostered numerous friendships. When presenting my academic credentials for Exeter, the primary grader remarked, "I don't know if you're a great student, but I know one thing, you're a hell of a tennis player." Additionally, I had an early reputation for seeking out jokes and making a concerted effort to elicit laughter. I made a conscious decision to sit next to the best teachers and make them laugh, despite my roommate's skepticism about investing time in laughter amid a rigorous schedule. I believed breaks in life, often found in unexpected places, were as crucial as dedicated schoolwork. If I could make others smile, it not only brightened their perspective but also made us wiser.

Although unfamiliar with squash, a racquet sport that came naturally to me, I approached the coach and declared, "I want to play on your team." Despite the coach's skepticism about my lack of prior experience, I started ranked #7 on the Princeton squash team and steadily improved. A defining moment occurred when I played the #1 player in the United States, hailing from the Naval Academy. Despite being two games to one behind, I employed psychological tactics, referencing my tennis victories. Ultimately, I won the match, briefly becoming the #1 player before settling at #2. The power of positive reinforcement, especially in adversity, became evident, even if fleeting. The school acknowledged that, had squash been a better-known sport, it would have been celebrated as one of the great comebacks.

One of the challenges at Princeton in my era was the mandatory bickering process. At that time, I roomed with a talented tennis player, #2 on the team. Bicker, a high-pressure activity, became overwhelming after several attempts. In a moment of frustration, I injected jokes, intending to lighten the atmosphere. Unfortunately, this backfired, as sincerity was highly valued during bicker evaluations. Despite being graded down, I managed to get into Cottage. A crucial decision arose when my roommate did not gain entry. I approached my second pick, offering to join their club if they accepted my roommate as well. They agreed, and in hindsight, it remains one of the decisions I am most proud of.

Bringing joy to others brought me immense happiness,

and I particularly enjoyed injecting humor into the track team's scores. However, I learned that such jests needed careful execution to avoid malicious intent. My advice to others considering such endeavors would be to approach it in the spirit of fun, ensuring you have your track shoes on when they become aware of your antics!

I had a habit of completing papers ahead of schedule, which sometimes annoyed my classmates. By getting ahead of a tight timetable, I believed I would benefit in the long run, a philosophy I aimed to carry forward in life. A valuable lesson unfolded on the last day of my art class. Having indulged in my first drinking experience in New York City, my final exam scores suffered. The art teacher, contemplating failing me, ultimately acknowledged my jokes and tennis skills, sparing me from a more severe outcome. This experience taught me enduring lessons about the impact of humor and its role as a savior in challenging times. While not always received with ease, humor has been my fortuitous companion, and I must confess, making others laugh has always brought me joy.

6 |

Starting My Career

After graduating from Princeton, I was fortunate to have a father who generously gifted me a convertible. He advised, "Do the best job you can at recruiting a beautiful woman, preferably a blonde." Early indications proved him right. I began my career at Manzanita Lodge, an all-male group of guys. I vividly recall telling the group, "What are we doing sitting around here? We should be out recruiting girls!" They responded, "Let's see what you do." Armed with determination, I pored over books showcasing undergraduates and spotted a beautiful blonde. I excitedly told my friends, "This is going to be a great date."

We attended a meeting where people ended up dancing with others before leaving, and to my surprise, the same woman was there. My roommates pointed her out, saying, "She's right over there." After downing another beer, I approached her, nearly knocking her date off his pillars. Eventually, he withdrew, and I seized the opportunity to dance with her. I confidently declared, "You know, I'm a great tennis player. I just beat someone who was #4 in the world." Her response was disheartening, "I don't like sports that much." My friends chided me, "What did you say? She just ran away from you." However, her roommates enjoyed my jokes and convinced Marianne, "You have to go out with this guy; he's very funny."

We attended a dance with many international students, where Marianne asked me, "What do you think of international?" I responded, "I love it; I didn't know anything about international." I used this as an excuse to send her postcards from various places. Eventually, she agreed to be pinned, signifying the next step towards engagement. However, I noticed she spent a significant amount of time with someone else from the business school, which annoyed me. Despite overcoming these troubles, we got engaged.

When people inquire about my major at Stanford, I always joke, "I majored in Marianne and took her out to a lot of places." Marianne's mother was never fond of me and suggested that Marianne should go to Germany for a year to learn more about the Danish and German languages. When Marianne broke this news to me, I was furious. As promised, I took her to Stanford by car but remained silent for three hours, later realizing it was one of the cruelest ways to impact someone. Slamming the car door, I left. This was one of the second-worst tricks one can play on somebody. Her roommate visited me, sharing that Marianne had done nothing but sob. I returned, made amends, and we eventually got married.

I'm not proud of this chapter, but Marianne and I were

married for 61 years. One thing that made Marianne fall in love with me was watching me play semi-professional tennis. I proposed to her on the early evening when I won the North Carolina tennis tournament.

7

The Contest

I had the opportunity to kickstart my career with Proctor and Gamble and Colgate Palmolive. Both companies rigorously evaluated my abilities to interact with people and impress individuals and organizations with my ideas. I distinctly remember the final interview with Proctor and Gamble. They congratulated me, stating that I had achieved the highest sales aptitude score they had ever seen. However, I expressed my desire not to go into sales but to pursue a career in advertising. Despite my reluctance, I eventually gave in for one summer and secured a significant position with P&G, overseeing the introduction of Mr. Clean throughout the state of Michigan.

In the first month, I received sharp feedback notes, all expressing uncertainty about my performance. Realizing the need for change, I gathered my peers and proposed a challenge, personally contributing some money. I felt suffocated by the standards they were advocating. The defining moment came at the end of a Friday when my group anxiously awaited the results. With cheers, I revealed the scores. Shortly after, I received a call from a higher-up at Proctor and Gamble, shocked at the transformation of my team. They had become one of the best in the nation. I had taken an off-the-record approach, creating a contest and awarding prizes, a strategy that proved successful. Though we didn't always top the charts, we consistently ranked near the top. The head salesman recognized my efforts and reassured me, "You're going to be all right, Jim, and also, you're funny. That doesn't hurt either."

Upon my return, colleagues urged me to practice interview skills. Colgate Palmolive became my practice interview, and to my surprise, I achieved the highest score. Colgate Palmolive offered me a position, considering my diverse background of attending 13 schools in 12 years as an ideal fit. Our first job with Colgate Palmolive International took us to Australia. In my initial days, I inadvertently used Aussie slang, resulting in laughter as I unknowingly asked a questionable question in their dialect. The Australians, known for their humor, embraced the opportunity to tease newcomers. Before leaving Australia, I shared a dream about a horse named Gadam Gadam winning a race. Remarkably, Gadam Gadam won the Melbourne Cup just as I had dreamt. At my farewell party, colleagues warned me against any future betting, emphasizing the unpredictable nature of such pursuits.

An important meeting in Australia, requiring me to take minutes for top-level executives, became a turning point. The minutes were near perfect, earning me a commendation from the vice president for the entire region. Despite only six months with the company, I was offered a significant promotion. The prospect of a move to Thailand emerged, presenting challenges as my wife had expected a relocation to Europe after our time in Australia.

The Thai Embassy cautioned me about the significant cultural differences, and I nervously approached Marianne with the news. After hours of discussion and tears, she reluctantly agreed to the move. As I drove to headquarters the next morning, doubts crept in about the impact on our family. At the office, I declined the promotion, choosing my wife over the firm. The vice president warned of regrets and potential consequences, emphasizing the financial sacrifice. Despite the fallout and freezing treatment from colleagues, a year later, I received an offer for a promotion to the subsidiary in Thailand.

My first task in Thailand involved developing a non-existent product, a solid detergent bar. With innovative promotional strategies, the product, Fab Detergent Bar, became a nationwide success. I later took a risky gamble in expanding a new product in Mexico, resulting in a substantial promotion and the challenge of learning a new language. However, my momentum faltered when I contracted pneumonia shortly after another promotion to the United States. A subsequent move to the head office in Greenwich, CT, introduced me to key figures, but my introduction was marred by fainting and a vaccination mishap.

8

Breaking Through

One of the most challenging personal decisions I faced was choosing between two job opportunities – one to stay in Mexico and the other to return to the United States. To involve the family in the decision- making process, I devised a little game. I explained the details of each job to my kids and asked them to contribute their thoughts. To add an element of interest, I crafted a test covering areas important to us, including some spiritual aspects. I informed everyone that I would reveal the decision after taking Marianne to dinner.

Despite Marianne's eagerness to know the outcome, I insisted on waiting until after our meal. After dinner, I tallied up the test answers, only to discover a dead even tie between the two options. Driving home, I felt a deep sense of indecision. In a moment of desperation, I raised my hands and said, "Lord, if you are there, tell me the answer, and I will follow You." Almost instantly, a voice from the radio seemed to suggest, "Turn it on, and you will have an answer."

I questioned the relevance, but the response came, "It will make sense later." The Coke jingle played, "You have to teach the world to sing in perfect harmony." Initially skeptical of a soda jingle, I was told, "You need to trust me more. My plan for you is to take the new job back in the United States. You have marvelous gifts, and I want you to reach out to as many people as you can."

Returning home, the kids anxiously awaited the decision. I emphasized that it was more about what the Lord wanted us to do. Over time, we saw the wisdom in the decision, but a significant obstacle emerged. Earlier that day, I had begun feeling weak and later fell seriously ill, requiring hospitalization. I struggled with deciding what to do. Sharing the revelation with my tennis mates, particularly those in Australia, received skepticism.

Seeking innovative approaches to family matters, I implemented a performance evaluation system that stirred controversy and negative feelings. I devised a test for each family member, assessing their performance on specific parameters I determined. Though my eldest son, Jim, harbors some resentment for this approach due to the distress it caused, it served as a quantitative means to ensure they did their best on their summer jobs.

9

Jon and Jim's Father and Son Tennis Championship

I may have made a mistake when I shared with my sons that my father and I had been ranked number two in the United States in Father and Son Tennis four times. I also mentioned my promise to my father about winning a father and son trophy with one of my sons. Unfortunately, our tennis journey did not start off well, as we were consistently in the back of the pack, far from winning any major tournaments.

In one particular championship, I played with my youngest son in the first round, which we lost in straight sets to a formidable team. Moving to the consolation round, we faced challenging conditions with heavy rain and a formidable opponent. The father was a good player, and the son was exceptional. While we lost the first round quite easily, we barely clinched the second. Then, something incredible happened during the third set. Facing match point against us, I made a small prayer, and my son, Jon, encouraged me, saying, "We can do it, Dad." In what felt like a mini-miracle, we saved seven consecutive match points and won the eighth. It was an unexpected victory that left Jon and me completely stunned. Although we lost easily in the next round, I called my father that evening to share our triumph, wishing he could have witnessed it.

The significance of the victory went beyond the match itself. I realized that I had never hugged any of my kids in such a manner before. Despite not being a historic match on paper, it held tremendous importance for both my son and me. The following year, we reached the semifinals of the national tournament, but it didn't compare to the impact of our first father and son victory.

Tennis, with its lessons, played a significant role in my life. I faced a former world number four on a cement court, a surface that brought out my best shots. We were evenly matched for the first two sets, and in the third set, I played exceptionally well. We reached match point for me, and as I hit a fast return on his hard serve, I threw my racquet in the air, anticipating a well-deserved win. However, my opponent contested the point, claiming I had taken the victory away from him. Despite his protests, I stood my ground, ensuring that this time, the victory was rightfully mine.

Reflecting on earlier incidents, I recalled matches taken away from me, particularly one in California during my time in business school. Playing against the second-ranked player in the world from India, I lost my composure due to questionable calls, ultimately leading to my defeat on the cement court, my favored surface.

10

The Importance of Humor

I have always found joy in making people laugh. A good friend once suggested, "Why don't you take a course on how to be a stand-up comic at the New School?" I pondered the idea and thought, "That would be great, I'd love that." The class consisted of about 15 people, and the teacher questioned a few times, "Are you sure you want to do this? You're a bit up there in age." I responded, "That's exactly why I want to do it. I have a history of people laughing at my jokes."

The final exam took place at a real comedy club, and I vividly remember shaking with fear as I stepped onto the stage. Despite my nerves, I did okay, and to my surprise, the teacher remarked, "You surprised me; you're actually pretty funny. Can you do another session?" I agreed, and while performing at the comedy club was a bit terrifying, I found joy in making people laugh. I wasn't a great comedian by any means, but I leveraged my age, leaving people shocked that I would take on such a challenge.

I always aimed to keep my humor clean, avoiding dirty jokes. While I didn't end up with a large audience, it made me feel good to face the challenge and bring laughter to those who were often amazed at my age.

11

Skydiving

I've always told my wife that I want to do some crazy things once I've fulfilled the task of giving each of my children a significant gift for their college stipend. One of the crazy things on my list was to go skydiving, despite my long-standing fear of heights. To prepare for this adventure, I read a book that advised taking it step by step.

To kick off the experience, I insisted that each of my children contribute to their college funds, following a sliding scale from 9th grade to just before college. This idea didn't sit well with my oldest son, who was put off by the requirement. In response, I offered a silly remark, suggesting it was a way for him to finance his own college education. My son Ray, however, was particularly enraged and handed over all his savings with frustration.

The day of skydiving finally arrived, and I found myself trembling as I approached the headquarters. To assess my readiness, they subjected me to a series of tests, including watching videos of various skydiving incidents, one of which resulted in a fatality. Although secretly hoping for rain that day, the weather was beautiful. Questions about my age were a common theme, with the head of the program expressing concern, asking if I was sure about going through with it. I insisted it was important, and before I knew it, I was boarding a small plane bound for 1500 feet above ground.

One young man before me showed visible signs of fear, and just as he began to panic, he declared he couldn't go through with it. Witnessing this, I found newfound strength to face the challenge. As I gradually worked through the pre-jump preparations, I observed experienced skydivers leaping from the plane. When it was my turn, my hands were shaking, but I didn't want to back out. I stood up, ready to take the plunge.

Thankfully, I didn't have to navigate the jump alone. The instructor assured me, "You'll be alright, just catch yourself off guard." Plunging 1500 feet from the plane, fear consumed me, and all I could do was pray. The entire descent was spent in prayer. The instructor reassured me that I had done the work and encouraged me to enjoy the remainder of the experience. Looking down, I saw others laughing and joking after completing their jumps. Landing with a thud on my rear end, I got up, screaming, "I did it!"

12

New York City Marathon

The second challenge I set for myself was running the New York City Marathon. The key to conquering a marathon is longevity and constantly affirming to yourself, "I can do this." In the year I participated, there were 35,000 people involved, and none of us were experts with PhDs in running.

The marathon is more about the mental test of convincing yourself you can endure and sticking with it. I ran throughout the parks in New York City, but a slight twist in the story occurred when I was unexpectedly chosen to run for Congress in New York City.

This unexpected turn of events came about whimsically when my nephew suggested, "You ought to consider running for Congress." I hesitated, citing my lack of experience. He encouraged me, saying, "Use that to entice them even more." Taking his advice, I entered the race and went through the interview process. There were few contenders since incumbents rarely lose, and I juggled the demands of marathon training along with this new endeavor.

It occurred to me that this political venture might give me an edge against my opponent was notably overweight. However, my primary focus remained on maintaining my marathon training, emphasizing the mental fortitude required to conquer such a significant physical challenge.

13

Campaign for Congress

My brother-in-law, a fervent follower of Republican politics, approached me and suggested, "You should try to run for Congress; there's an opening." Skeptical about my lack of experience, I hesitated, but he urged me to embrace risks, a sentiment I often preached. On the last day for congressional nominations from the Upper East Side, I appeared before a room with seven or eight individuals monitoring potential candidates.

They instructed me to make a compelling case for why I should represent the Upper East Side in Congress. Undeterred, I adopted a rudimentary approach, creating a crude brochure. Drawing on my background in public speaking, I confidently presented my case and was surprised when they named me one of the finalists. My kids, initially thinking it was a joke, questioned my candidacy due to my lack of experience. Shockingly, I was selected as one of the two finalists and instructed to show up early in the morning for a final decision.

Starting at 8 am at the Republican headquarters in Brooklyn, I encountered a man who could barely stand, realizing he was intoxicated. Despite this, I had a positive meeting with his wife, a tennis fan who recognized my national ranking. Later that day, the organizer informed me that I was their candidate, emphasizing my favorable outcome in Brooklyn. Thus began the door-to-door canvassing phase of my campaign, enduring insults, thrown objects, and even subway confrontations.

Securing enough signatures to qualify for the ballot, I simultaneously prepared for the New York City Marathon. The following week, I officially entered the race with my family incredulous at the turn of events. Running for office proved to be a challenging endeavor, testing my resilience amid humorous opportunities and attempts to derail my campaign with fake addresses and disruptive encounters.

On election night, seeing my name regularly flash on the screen was surreal. Despite receiving only a handful of votes, a result consistent with others challenging incumbents, The New York Times acknowledged me as a very articulate candidate. While the campaign proved to be one of the more interesting chapters of my life, I recognized that politics was not my calling.

14

Overcoming Cancer

My wife and I celebrated 61 years of marriage, a milestone that brought profound joy to our lives. However, about six months later, my joy turned to concern when I received a diagnosis of colon cancer with a severity rating of 4.4 out of 5.

In the face of this challenging news, my daughter Jennifer, a relentless advocate for my health, came across an article about a physician who claimed to have found a potential cure for colon cancer. This doctor conducted a small test, demonstrating complete remission in his pilot group of 20 patients within six months, using a new drug. Jennifer, determined and persuasive, brought this breakthrough to my attention, insisting that I explore this potential solution.

Through Jennifer's tenacity and her relentless efforts to advocate for my inclusion in the trial, I became the subject for the next experimental treatment. She passionately conveyed the urgency of my situation, pushing for my participation. After an intense campaign, Jennifer informed me that, against the odds, I secured a slot on the last day of the trial. In a final interview with the head doctor, he regretfully stated that they were out of time, citing that my file didn't align perfectly with their criteria.

Employing my humor as a weapon, I remarked that, if he had an interest in tennis, I once defeated Arthur Ashe and would be delighted to offer him a lesson or two. Surprisingly, the doctor found my approach unusual and intriguing. He took time to reconsider and eventually returned with the welcome news that I was accepted into the trial. He even offered to become my personal physician.

Today, I am on the verge of being declared cancer-free, a testament to the power of prayer, perseverance, and the miracles that can unfold even in the face of adversity. This experience reinforced the lesson that, no matter how dire circumstances may seem, resilience and faith can lead to remarkable outcomes.

15

Petey Greene

My mornings usually began with the soothing cadence of my wife quoting or reflecting on lessons from the Bible. One early morning, she posed a question that would alter the course of our lives. "Jim, I'd like you to help me with something," she said. Emerging from my groggy state, I listened as she revealed her contemplation of a career in the ministry. "What would you think if I said I want to be a minister?" she asked. Overwhelmed with emotion, I responded, "You know, I always thought you should."

Marianne's decision to enroll in Princeton Theological Seminary left me facing an unexpected crossroads. While delighted for her, the realization struck that I would now navigate life on my own. Seeking solace and direction, I visited the public library to ponder my options. Serendipitously, a stranger approached, asking if I could read something to help her. Our conversation revealed a shared desire to make a positive impact.

Inspired by this encounter, I observed a group with a Bible and considered whether God was steering me toward a role involving the scriptures. Engaging with the church community, I explored opportunities to contribute. That evening, I proposed to Marianne the idea of aiding prison inmates in developing essential skills through the teachings of the Bible. After a visit to a local prison, the enthusiastic warden embraced the concept, envisioning literacy and even degrees for the inmates.

With Marianne's support, I initiated a pilot program, driving a small group to the prison for trial sessions. As the results approached, nervous anticipation set in. I called Marianne to be by my side as we tallied the responses. The outcome was beyond my expectations – every participant expressed positivity and a desire to continue. The program had found its footing. Further expanding the initiative, my dedicated friend volunteered to assist, and our efforts resonated not just within the prison but also with nearby schools. The program gained momentum, involving 1500 students across the East Coast.

Reflecting on this journey, the undeniable truth surfaced – God had orchestrated transformative change in my life. A message from the President of Princeton acknowledged the program's impact, assuring its lasting legacy. As I celebrate these achievements in my late 80s, the adventure continues, in the belief that God keeps opening doors for new beginnings.

Memories through the Years

Jim and Marianne's Wedding

Wedding

Jim and Marianne's Wedding

Jim and Marianne at Princeton
University's P-rade

Jim Accepting an Award from
Princeton University

Princeton

Children

With daughters Jenny and Melody

With sons Jim, Jonathan, and Ray

Sons Ray, Jim, and Jonathan

Sons

Jim and Ray

Daughters Jenny and Melody

Daughters

Jenny

Grandchildren

Grandchildren

Children and Grandchildren at the
Peacock Inn

With Marianne at the Law Offices
of James Scott Farrin

The Law Offices of James Scott Farrin

With son Jim at the Law Offices of
James Scott Farrin's 25th
Anniversary

With Charlie Puttkammer

AARP Awards Ceremony

With Family Accepting AARP
Purpose Prize Award

AARP Purpose Prize

2017 AARP Purpose Prize with the Petey Greene Program

When Jim Farrin wrote his college thesis, he never could have imagined that the topic he chose would have real significance in his life more than 50 years later.

"I wrote my senior thesis at Princeton on Judge Benjamin Barr Lindsey, who, in the early 20th century, did not believe in incarceration for youthful offenders."

After graduation, Judge Lindsey faded into Jim's past as he moved forward into a business career in the private sector. Still, Jim says, over the years, he always thought it would be great to be able to give back and have a strong mission as the centerpiece of his next career.

Then came the phone call...with an offer that Jim couldn't refuse.

"This is the best job that I have ever had, working for a cause we tremendously believe in!"

Prior to Petey Greene, Jim spent the majority of his career in international marketing management with several high-profile, retail companies including Colgate Palmolive International and The Mennen Company.

Right before he changed careers again, he found out that his wife of 61 years was dying and eventually passed away. Shortly after, he fought multiple bouts of cancer and is proud to say he beat them all. With God on your side, there's no limit.